D0689803

Looking at . . . Parasaurolophus

A Dinosaur from the CRETACEOUS Period

THE NEW
DINOSAUR
COLLECTION

For a free color catalog describing Gareth Stevens' list of high-quality books, call 1-800-542-2595 (USA) or 1-800-461-9120 (Canada). Gareth Stevens' Fax: (414) 225-0377.

Library of Congress Cataloging-in-Publication Data

Coleman, Graham, 1963-
  Looking at— Parasaurolophus / written by Graham Coleman; illustrated by Tony Gibbons.
    p. cm. — (The New dinosaur collection)
  Includes index.
  ISBN 0-8368-1086-4
  1. Parasaurolophus—Juvenile literature. [1. Parasaurolophus. 2.
Dinosaurs.] I. Gibbons, Tony, ill. II. Title. III. Series.
QE862.065C65   1994
567.9'7—dc20   93-37052

This North American edition first published in 1994 by
Gareth Stevens Publishing
1555 North RiverCenter Drive, Suite 201
Milwaukee, Wisconsin 53212 USA

This U.S. edition © 1994 by Gareth Stevens, Inc. Created with original © 1993 by
Quartz Editorial Services, Premier House, 112 Station Road, Edgware HA8 7AQ U.K.

Consultant: Dr. David Norman, Director of the Sedgwick Museum of Geology,
University of Cambridge, England.

Additional artwork by Clare Heronneau.

Printed in the United States of America

 3 4 5 6 7 8 9 9 99 98 97 96 95

Looking at . . . Parasaurolophus
A Dinosaur from the CRETACEOUS Period

by Graham Coleman

Illustrated by Tony Gibbons

THE NEW
DINOSAUR
COLLECTION

Gareth Stevens Publishing
MILWAUKEE

Contents

Introducing
Parasaurolophus

Parasaurolophus was a plant-eating dinosaur that ate twigs and leaves.

Parasaurolophus
(PAR-A-SAUR-OH-LOAF-US) was a duck-billed dinosaur with an unusual, tubelike crest on its head. It lived about 74 million years ago during the Late Cretaceous Period in the part of the world that is now North America.

This dinosaur generally walked on its two back legs, but it had strong arms. This meant it could have walked on all fours sometimes. It may also have used its arms for swimming.

It had hundreds of small teeth with sharp cutting edges that it used for chewing food.

How did **Parasaurolophus** use its tubelike crest? And how did it spend its day? Turn the pages that follow and learn all about this fascinating dinosaur.

5

Harmless

Many other dinosaurs were much bigger than **Parasaurolophus**.

But it would have seemed enormous if you could have stood next to it. **Parasaurolophus** grew to a length of 33 feet (10 meters).

6

Hadrosaur

Parasaurolophus was as long as three cars. It had a short neck and quite a large head.

The male's head crest alone grew up to 6 feet (1.8 m) long — the height of an average man. The female's crest, however, was much shorter.

But, unlike ducks, **Hadrosaurs** had rows of teeth that they used for grinding food.

Their beaks were strong and sharp, more like those of turtles or tortoises. They used them for tearing off shoots and leaves from the plants they ate.

Hadrosaurs' bodies were all fairly similar, but their heads evolved into a wide variety of shapes.

Parasaurolophus was one of the duck-billed dinosaurs known as **Hadrosaurs** that began to appear in the middle of the Cretaceous Period about 90 million years ago.

Hadrosaurs all had in common a beak that looked a little like a duck's bill.

Parasaurolophus had a large, sturdy body, but it did not have any thumb spikes or a clubbed tail with which to defend itself.

Its strong arms and legs meant that it was quite mobile, however, and it was probably able to run very fast to escape from predators.

Striking skeleton

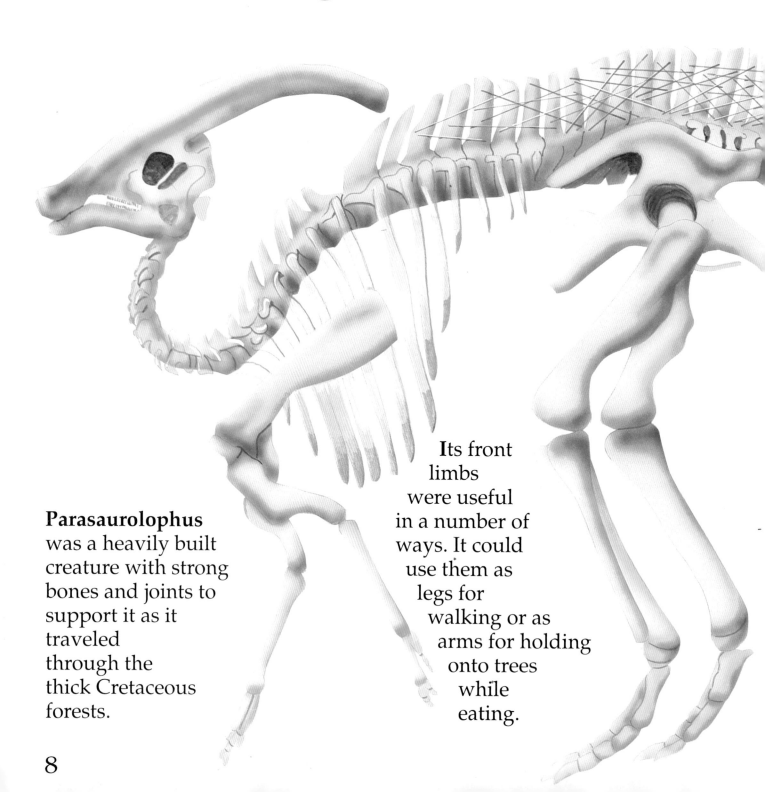

Parasaurolophus was a heavily built creature with strong bones and joints to support it as it traveled through the thick Cretaceous forests.

Its front limbs were useful in a number of ways. It could use them as legs for walking or as arms for holding onto trees while eating.

Parasaurolophus's hands were flat and shaped like paddles. Scientists believe the hands could also help the dinosaur swim.

Its back legs were much longer than its front limbs.

So its ankle and toe bones had to be powerful enough to support all its weight. Parasaurolophus weighed about three tons — as much as an adult elephant does today.

At the front of its mouth was a beak used to snip off plants. Parasaurolophus also had hundreds of small, diamond-shaped teeth lining its upper and lower jaws. They formed a large surface that acted like a chopping board.

Because it spent so much time chewing its food to help its digestion, Parasaurolophus's teeth wore down quite often, but they continuously grew back.

The most spectacular feature of Parasaurolophus's body was the crest on its head. Scientists once thought it was used as a snorkel for breathing under the water. But further study showed there was no opening in the crest, so this was not possible.

Like most other Hadrosaurs, Parasaurolophus had a network of bony tendons among the bones that pointed up from its spine. The tendons were especially strong around the dinosaur's hip bones.

The long, thin bones that pointed down from Parasaurolophus's tail gave this dinosaur the strength to balance on its tail when it reared up on its back legs to eat. It also had good control over its tail, which was useful if the dinosaur needed it for a weapon.

Cretaceous times

When **Parasaurolophus** lived, during the Late Cretaceous Period, there was a wide variety of trees and other plants — magnolia, laurel, and poplar trees, for instance — growing on our planet.

So this crested creature would not have been bored with its diet. The contents of one **Parasaurolophus**'s fossilized stomach, for instance, contained conifer twigs, along with a variety of needles and seeds.

Footprints have been found that show how duck-billed dinosaurs like **Parasaurolophus** moved around in herds. They had good eyesight, sharp hearing, a strong sense of smell, and the ability to swim.

This made them among the most intelligent and advanced of all the dinosaurs.

Like all the dinosaurs that were alive in the Late Cretaceous Period, **Parasaurolophus** died out 65 million years ago. There are many theories about their extinction. The most likely explanation is that a giant meteorite hit Earth, blotting out the Sun and making the survival of the dinosaurs impossible. However, many other creatures survived. Among them were frogs, birds, mammals, and some types of fish.

Mysterious crest

When scientists first studied the remains of **Parasaurolophus**, they could not agree on the purpose of its crest.

Inside the crest were four thin tubes. Two of them went up the crest, and two went down. If **Parasaurolophus** breathed out strongly, it could make a low bellowing sound (like a foghorn) through its crest.

Another theory suggested that the dinosaur's crest could be adjusted to rest against the back of its neck. This might have helped **Parasaurolophus** run through the thick forest without getting its crest caught in vegetation.

One idea was that the crest acted like a snorkel for use under the water. If this was true, the tubes in the crest could have been used as tanks for storing air. But it was not.

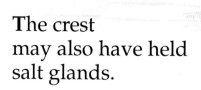

The crest may also have held salt glands.

Many present-day reptiles have similar glands near their noses or eyes. These are used to keep a healthy salt balance in their bodies. Scientists also noticed that the tubes in the crest were linked to **Parasaurolophus**'s nostrils. Perhaps it had an incredibly powerful sense of smell.

All of these theories are difficult to prove. But there seems little doubt that **Parasaurolophus** was able to make sounds by blowing air through its crest.

One scientist constructed a model of **Parasaurolophus**'s crest and blew air through it, making a deep sound. One thing is for certain — the Cretaceous forests would have been noisy places with herds of **Parasaurolophus** around!

Swimming

It was a hot afternoon some 74 million years ago. A young **Parasaurolophus** had wandered away from its family to explore a new part of the Cretaceous forest.

It caught sight of a herd of **Parasaurolophus**, but there were too many of them, and they were too far away. The giant meat-eater was not good at a long chase.

It was lazily browsing, nibbling at some tasty-looking plants that grew by a lake. Meanwhile, a huge and hungry **Tyrannosaurus rex** (TIE-<u>RAN</u>-OH-<u>SAW</u>-RUS <u>RECKS</u>) was hunting for a meal.

It preferred to launch an attack from a short distance. It changed direction and headed toward the lake.

Suddenly, the young **Parasaurolophus** heard a sound from another part of the forest.

14

to safety

It recognized the sound as a warning from another member of its family. The crested dinosaur lifted its head and looked around. At that moment, **Tyrannosaurus rex** came crashing through the bushes. It gave a mighty roar and headed for its victim.

But if it did not do something quickly, it was going to be in terrible danger. It plunged into the lake. **Tyrannosaurus rex** followed, but it was not a good swimmer.

Parasaurolophus stood rooted to the spot. It knew it was no fighter and could not see a way past the fearsome creature that was coming closer.

Tyrannosaurus rex struggled back to shallow water. The young **Parasaurolophus** escaped, and it soon rejoined its family.

Weird and wonderful heads

From its skeletal remains, we know

No other dinosaur had such an impressive crest, although many dinosaurs had other unusual features on their heads.

Pachycephalosaurus (PAK-EE-KEF-AL-OH-SAW-RUS) **(2)**, for example, had a bony, dome-shaped head about 24 inches (60 centimeters) long, ideal for head-butting fights.

Parasaurolophus (1) had a rather ordinary body, for a dinosaur.

1

It did not have interesting features such as a long neck, plates along its back, or a tail-club. But the shape of its head, with its curved crest that scientists think was up to 6 feet (1.8 m) long, makes this dinosaur look different from many others.

2

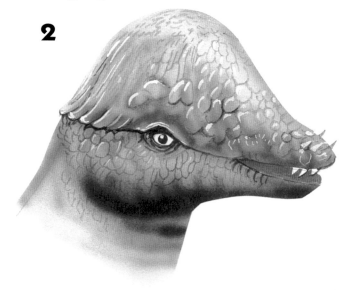

Styracosaurus (<u>STY</u>-RAK-OH-<u>SAW</u>-RUS) **(3)** was a heavily built creature that resembled its more famous relative, **Triceratops** (TRY-<u>SER</u>-A-TOPS).

3

Styracosaurus had a long skull surrounded by an impressive frill. There were six spines rising from its frill, and its nose had one sharp horn. Notice that the longest spines were at the top of the frill. This is why it was given a name meaning "spiked lizard." From the tip of its snout to the end of the longest frill, its head measured 6-1/2 feet (2 m).

Styracosaurus looked very frightening, and few dinosaurs would have dared attack it. The spikes may also have been used to ward off rivals of the same species.

The nose horn was probably used as a weapon for defense against enemies or rivals of the same species. As you can see, it pointed straight upward.

Notice, too, how the spines of **Styracosaurus** were shortest at the sides and longest at the top.

Shamosaurus (<u>SHAM</u>-OH-<u>SAW</u>-RUS) **(4)** was an armored dinosaur that lived in early Cretaceous times in what is now Mongolia. Its name means "Gobi reptile." It was so called because its remains were first found in 1983 in the Gobi Desert. Its head was tough and fierce-looking, with spikes just behind and to the sides of the eyes for protection.

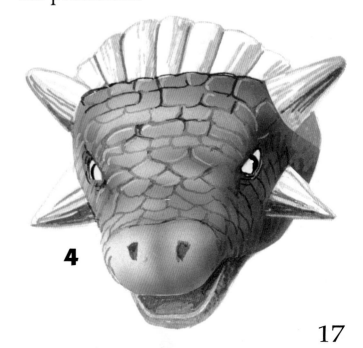

4

Scientists have to do a lot of work before a dinosaur skeleton can be assembled and ready for a museum.

When scientists receive the bones of a dinosaur, their very first job is to take the bones out of their protective packaging. This must be done very carefully.

Next, the bones have to be removed from the casing of rock in which they usually are embedded.

This is done using a variety of instruments that range from small needles and chisels to machines that blow air at the rock.

laboratory

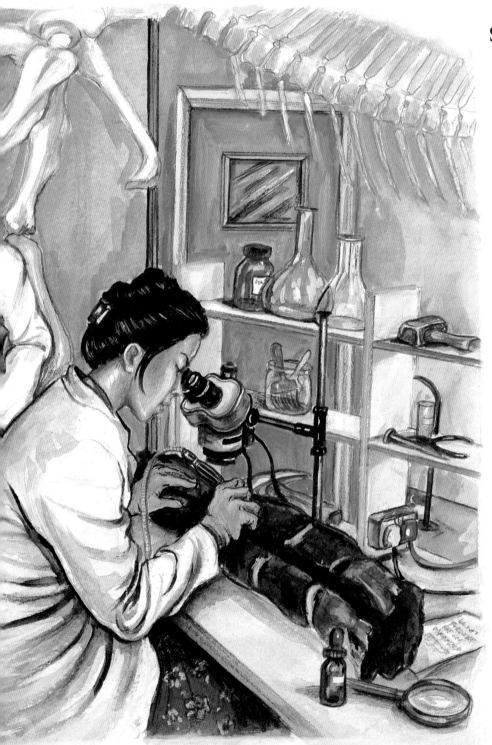

Sometimes the bones must also be treated with chemicals to preserve them. After having been buried in the ground for so many millions of years, they can easily be damaged by exposure to the air and rough handling.

Scientists also number all the bones. They must make many notes and drawings before reassembling the bones.

Finally, the bones are fitted together and mounted on a base so the skeleton stands up. There are dinosaur skeletons in natural history museums throughout the world.

Parasaurolophus and cousins

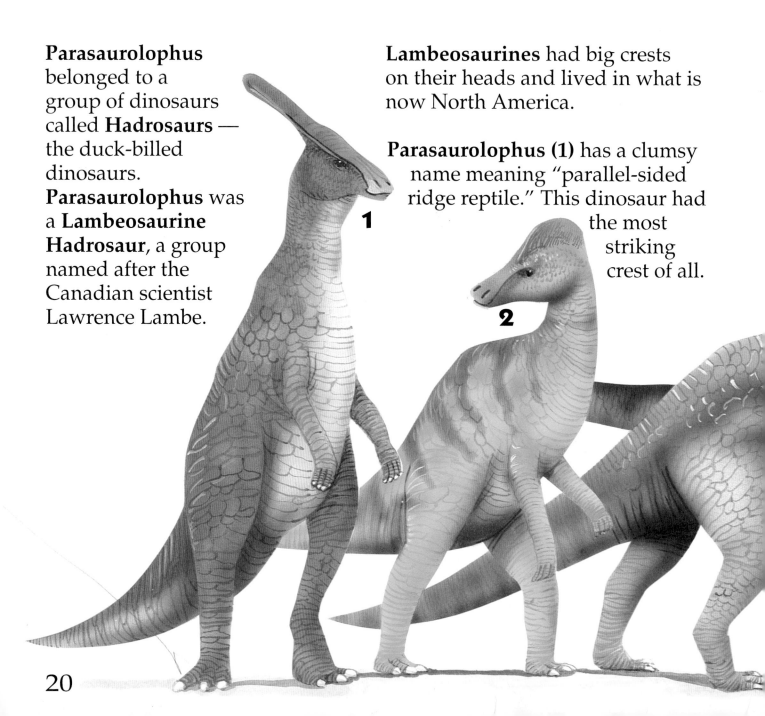

Parasaurolophus belonged to a group of dinosaurs called **Hadrosaurs** — the duck-billed dinosaurs. **Parasaurolophus** was a **Lambeosaurine Hadrosaur**, a group named after the Canadian scientist Lawrence Lambe.

Lambeosaurines had big crests on their heads and lived in what is now North America.

Parasaurolophus (1) has a clumsy name meaning "parallel-sided ridge reptile." This dinosaur had the most striking crest of all.

Hypacrosaurus (HIE-PAK-ROE-SAW-RUS) **(2)** has an unusual name, meaning "below the top reptile." It was a large duck-billed dinosaur that grew to about 30 feet (9 m) long, the length of a bus. **Hypacrosaurus**'s crest was more rounded than those of its close relatives.

Corythosaurus (KO-RITH-OH-SAW-RUS) **(3)** had a thin crest that looked like a plate. Inside this crest was a system of breathing tubes that was connected to its nostrils and mouth.

Scientists think **Corythosaurus** may have been able to make hooting noises using these tubes.

Another member of this family was **Lambeosaurus** (LAM-BEE-OH-SAW-RUS) **(4)**. Its name means "Lambe's reptile." It, too, lived in Late Cretaceous times. Its crest was an odd shape and pointed forward. Like **Corythosaurus**, **Lambeosaurus** may have been able to produce noises. It was bigger than its relatives — about 50 feet (15 m) long.

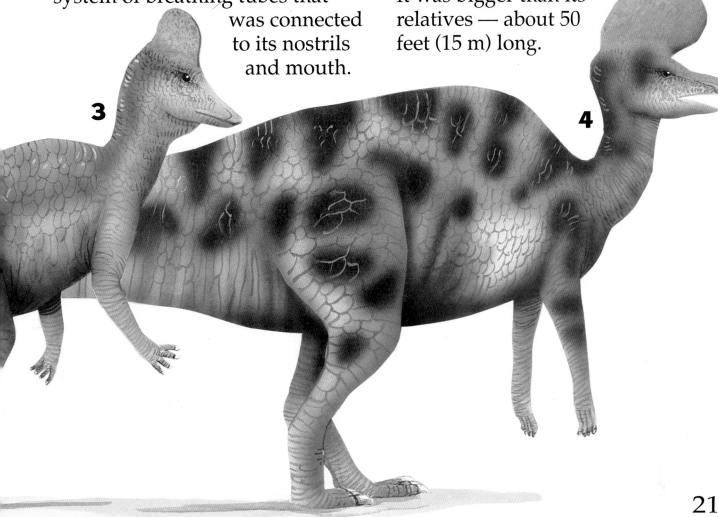

21

Parasaurolophus data

Since its remains were first discovered, there has been a great deal of argument about the way **Parasaurolophus** lived during its time on our planet. Much of it has concerned the purpose of its amazing crest. But equally interesting are questions about its sense of smell, hearing, and eyesight, as well as its ability to swim or wade through water.

Scientific study of its remains seems to show that **Parasaurolophus** is likely to have been a very advanced and intelligent animal.

Bony crests

Many dinosaurs had unusual head features, but none of them had anything quite as magnificent as **Parasaurolophus**'s crest. The females did not have crests as large as the males. Scientists think this is because the males used their crests to attract females during the mating season.

Sharp eyesight

The best clue to **Parasaurolophus**'s eyesight is its eye sockets. These were very large for a dinosaur, and so it must have had big eyes. Scientists believe this means it had very sharp eyesight. **Parasaurolophus** had eyes on either side of its head and was very tall, so it could have seen quite a ways on both sides. There is no reason why it should not have been able to see in color as well.

Strong arms

Parasaurolophus could walk upright or on all fours. Its front arms were not as long as the back ones, but they were very strong and had four "fingers." It could have used them for holding onto trees while eating or even for paddling through water.

Acute hearing

Parasaurolophus had a thin ear bone at the back of its skull. This bone was very sensitive to sound, so this dinosaur probably had excellent hearing.

GLOSSARY

beak — the hard parts of a bird's mouth; a bill.

conifers — woody shrubs or trees that bear their seeds in cones.

crest — a growth on top of an animal's head.

evolve — to change shape or develop gradually over a long period of time.

extinction — the dying out of all members of a plant or animal species.

fossils — traces or remains of plants and animals found in rock.

frill — a fringe or ruffle around the neck of an animal.

herd — a group of animals that travels together.

mate — to join together to produce young.

meteorite — a chunk of rock from space that reaches Earth before burning up completely.

predators — animals that kill other animals for food.

remains — a dead body or corpse.

snorkel — a curved breathing tube swimmers use when they are just beneath the water's surface.

tendon — a strong band of tissue that connects a muscle to a bone.

INDEX